Milkweed Visitors

by Mary Holland

Bas Relief Publishing Group
and
Monarchs in the Classroom

*To Sadie,
my favorite
milkweed visitor*

Text and photographs
© Mary Holland 2006
All Rights Reserved

Published by
Bas Relief Publishing Group
P.O. Box 426, Glenshaw, PA 15116
in cooperation with
Monarchs in the Classroom
University of Minnesota,
Department of Fisheries, Wildlife and Conservation Biology
1980 Folwell Ave
St. Paul MN 55108

ISBN-13: 978-0-9657472-4-0
ISBN-10: 0-9657472-4-7
Library of Congress Control Number: 2005934214

No part of this book may be reproduced or transmitted in any form or by any means, electronic or mechanical, including photocopying, recording or by any storage and retrieval system, without permission from the publisher.

Have you ever visited a milkweed patch?

When you do, be sure to look very closely. You may find someone looking back at you!

Milkweed plants have many visitors who come in many different shapes and sizes.

Before meeting some of these visitors, let's learn a few things about milkweed plants.

Do you know how milkweed got its name?

Milkweed has white sap inside its leaves and stem that looks like milk.

Like other plants called weeds, milkweed grows wild in many places.

Most of us have seen the silky seeds that burst out of milkweed pods in the fall.

Did you know that all the milkweed seeds in a pod come from one milkweed flower?

To make seeds, milkweed flowers need insects to move pollen from one flower to another. This is called pollination. The sweet smell of the flowers and the nectar in each of the five cups attracts the insects.

The cups are the perfect size for a ladybug when it is not busy being a fierce predator!

Pollen is found in tiny sacs tucked into the center of the milkweed flower. The sacs stick to the visiting insects' legs. Sometimes bees eat the pollen, but often it is left behind on another milkweed flower that the bee visits. Bees are important pollinators that help flowers make seeds.

Look for the yellow pollen sacs on the tips of the honeybee's legs.

Nectar attracts the great spangled fritillary butterfly to milkweed flowers.

The name for an insect that drinks nectar is nectivore.

A butterfly's long tongue is called a proboscis. It is used like a straw to sip nectar from flowers.

This eastern tiger swallowtail butterfly ate leaves from trees and shrubs when it was a caterpillar.

As a butterfly, it drinks nectar from milkweed and many other flowers.

Honeybees visit milkweed flowers because they find good things to eat and drink in the blossoms. This honeybee is collecting nectar to store in her hive. Bees turn the nectar into honey which they will eat during the winter, when there are no flowers or nectar.

Like honeybees, bumblebees feed on nectar and pollen. They are important pollinators too.

This yellow jacket is a nectivore, but she is a predator too. She chews up insects to feed her young.

A monarch butterfly drinks nectar from many plants, but she always lays her eggs on milkweed. Tiny caterpillars hatch from the eggs. First a monarch caterpillar eats its egg shell and then it starts eating milkweed leaves.

As monarch caterpillars grow, milkweed is the only food they will eat. Because they eat plants, we call them herbivores.

This caterpillar is about ten days old.

Japanese beetles are herbivores that eat both milkweed leaves and flowers. They find plants to eat by sensing them with their feelers, or antennae.

Can you find this beetle's two antennae? They look like little forks coming out of its head.

Milkweed longhorn beetles eat milkweed and have long antennae that look like horns. When they are young, they live underground and eat milkweed roots. As adults they crawl up out of the soil and eat milkweed leaves.

Groups of milkweed tussock moth caterpillars are often found munching on milkweed leaves. They get their name from the tufts or tussocks on their body that make them look like little mops.

Look for tussock moth caterpillars whenever you see milkweed plants that have been nearly stripped of their leaves.

Milkweed bugs are herbivores that especially like milkweed pods and seeds. Sometimes you can find many young milkweed bugs together on milkweed pods.

Some insects are predators. They come to milkweed plants to find other insects to eat. This robber fly sits on milkweed leaves while it watches for dinner to fly by. Once it catches an insect, the robber fly uses its long pointed beak to suck liquid from inside the insect.

Dragonflies are predators that often rest on milkweed. They hold their bristly legs together like a net to catch other insects in mid-air.

This dragonfly may return to its milkweed perch to eat its prey.

An adult potter wasp drinks nectar, but when it is time to lay eggs she becomes a predator.

First, she makes a little mud pot.

Then she goes hunting for caterpillars.

The potter wasp stuffs the caterpillars she catches into the pot. She then lays an egg in it and closes the opening with mud.

When the egg hatches, the young potter wasp eats the caterpillars before it chews its way out of the pot.

Some spiders hide in the milkweed flowers where they wait to surprise and catch their meals. This honeybee didn't see the white crab spider waiting for it. Did you?

The black and yellow garden spider spins sticky, silk webs to catch insects. A milkweed patch is a good place to spin a web, because there are so many insect visitors.

When an insect gets caught, the spider wraps it in silk so it can't get away.

Ants can be nectivores, predators and even farmers! These ants are tending tiny insects called aphids. The aphids drink sap from milkweed leaves and the ants protect them from predators. When the ants stroke the aphids with their antennae, the aphids release a sweet liquid called honeydew which the ants drink.

Some insects come to the milkweed patch to have a bite to eat, some to have a drink and some, like this katydid, simply come to have a rest.

What visitors have you seen in a milkweed patch?

Milkweed Patch Vocabulary

ANTENNAE — Antennae are sense organs on the heads of insects and some of their relatives, sometimes called feelers. Antennae are used to smell and to sense air motion, heat and sound.

CATERPILLAR — Many insects have four stages in their life cycle: egg, larva, pupa and adult. The larval stage of a butterfly or moth is called a caterpillar. It has eating mouthparts and feeds on plants.

FERTILIZE — In many animals and plants a new individual is made when tiny cells from two different individuals join together. In plants this happens when pollen joins, or fertilizes, an egg cell to make a seed.

HERBIVORE — Herbivores are animals that eat plants.

HONEY — Honey is a liquid, sweeter and thicker than nectar, that is made by honeybees from nectar.

LARVA — Larva is the name for the second stage in the life cycle of many insects—after the egg. Larvae can be called many other names. In butterflies and moths they're called caterpillars, in beetles they're called grubs, and in flies they're called maggots.

NECTAR — Nectar is a sweet liquid produced by some flowers to attract insects.

NECTIVORE — Nectivores are animals whose diet consists mainly of nectar.

POLLEN — Pollen is a fine powder, produced by flowers, that fertilizes seeds. Pollen can be carried by animals or by the wind.

POLLINATION — Pollinaation is the transfer of pollen from the male to the female parts of a flower.

PREDATOR — Predators are animals that eat other animals

PROBOSCIS — A proboscis is an insect mouth part that works like a straw. Adult insects use proboscises to suck nectar and other liquids. In some insects, like butterflies, the proboscis is coiled under the head when it is not being used.

Photograph by Medora Hebert

Mary Holland is a naturalist, nature photographer and natural history columnist who lives near a milkweed patch in Vermont. She has worked in the field of environmental education her entire life, sharing her curiosity about and appreciation of the natural world with people of all ages. She and her daughter, Sadie, have had many pets, including Hickory the hedgehog, Wilbur the wood turtle, Nigel the parrot, Steamer the guinea pig, Timmy Willy the mouse, Tessa the tarantula, Gertie the garter snake, Buddy G the leopard gecko and many other wild and not so wild pets, including Hazel the basset hound. Both Sadie and Hazel can be found inside the covers of this author's first children's book, **Milkweed Visitors**.

For more information about the milkweed patch or to get involved in a citizen science project monitoring a milkweed patch near you visit:

Monarchs in the Classroom at:
http://www.monarchlab.org

and

The Monarch Larva Monitoring Project at:
http://www.mlmp.org